Accessing Your Intuition Workbook

A DAILY WORKBOOK TO CREATE AN INTUITIVE FOUNDATION AND LIVE AN ENLIGHTENED LIFE

BY KIR NOEL - MEDICAL INTUITIVE

My teacher- Rev. Ellen Resch

Accessing Your Intuition Workbook

We all have a drop of wisdom to bring. Seek yours, even if it has become deeply buried.

Kir Noel

Table of Contents

Kir Noel

FOREWARD

Lucky you, the workbook you're about to read is written by a true healer. Kir is an inspiring teacher who's been a student of Buddhism for four decades, in addition to living a sober life for almost the same amount of time. She teaches me every day, by the way she lives her life with kindness and her desire to always give back. She continues to teach me the importance of being present. How the practice of forgiveness and letting go is a way to heal, to grow into who we're meant to be and that when we're clear and present and able to be quiet, without distraction, it allows us to access our innermost selves. Our intuitive selves…Our true selves….

If you follow Kir's workbook, the only thing that I can guarantee, is you'll take a journey of self-discovery and as Kir would say, "wherever that journey takes you, will ultimately be up to you."

Angela English

DEDICATION

My teacher, Reverend Ellen Resch

My partner, Angela English

My children

Mom and dad – Maxine and Larry

My AA Community

The Tibetan Kagyu Lineage and the K.T.D. Monastery

My guides and higher forces that direct my life.

1-FINDING YOUR CLARITY

In this one lifetime, can you have the realization of your innate nature and personal path; the answer is yes. We all seek fulfillment, peace, and happiness within ourselves. Often, we're only able to discover this when we've experienced tragedy, such as the death of a loved one, an illness, or a traumatic event. Then suddenly, almost instantly, we awaken to a new perspective. Life's earthquakes can become the catalyst to reclaiming our direction, that we couldn't otherwise find. You may find yourself asking why am I here, what am I here to do? If you're seeking these answers, then this booklet is a simple direct path, to follow. As you apply the exercises here, you will build your foundation. The result will be an elevated consciousness, a path to your clearer self. It is a place to connect beyond your ego.

Transformation comes from taking direct personal action. If you're lucky enough to have a life where you have the time and desire to search, you have what is required to find this. New awareness's will come to you as you do this daily foundation building process. My heartfelt wish for you is that no matter where you are in your life, you may find a way that speaks to you, and you will seek your clear self.

I was adopted at ten months old after being in foster care. I was the second child to be adopted into our family of three children, all from different families. Being the middle child, I always felt a keen sense of responsibility for others. For the first decade of my life, I was taught by my mom to believe in myself. She was forty when she adopted me and very much wanted children. I received the message form her that I was valuable and deserving of love. I credit this early parenting and nurturing with why I transcended what I went through for the rest my childhood. By my tenth birthday, my mom was an active alcoholic, and both my siblings were heavily using drugs. My father worked all the time and when he was around, he wasn't emotionally available. The events I witnessed, triggered feelings of mistrust and fear, as a response to my life.

In my early twenties, I became aware of my need to change from the inside out. It was at this time that I met a spiritual Buddhist teacher Reverend Ellen Resch. Studying with her, I began to understand how my primary thoughts were projections of my childhood fears. As I learned about myself, I developed a structure that is the basis of this booklet. It required me doing a five-minute, twice a day, self-observation, and meditation process.

In the beginning of my practice, I encountered all my old patterns and reactions. So, I started this, stopped, and started again, despite my resistance. I began to transform. Change is always a struggle within us. Because I saw the rewards while doing this, I was finally able to make a commitment to myself and to the practice.

The basis of my stability and clarity was found doing the steps that came out of these trainings. I discovered the patterns learned from my childhood blocked me from myself.

I learned to discern when my thoughts were coming from my ego mind vs. my intuitive mind. Creating this distinction, allowed me to stop reacting to the parts of myself which were and are still able to respond out of the fears that I hold from my childhood trauma. This became the structure of how I built a foundation. In my case it was a journey of taking down my defenses, brick by brick.

I could see the calmer part of me, and I connected to my intuition. This allowed me to develop a life working, professionally, as a medical intuitive. I also continue to find forgiveness for myself and others. My old self judgement has been resolved, not to say that it doesn't reappear regarding the now. When I feel my fear or my inner critic in the present moment, I can look at myself through the lens of my intuition.

We're all unique spiritual beings, each deserving of unconditional love. In my view, we each hold a piece of a complex organic puzzle. If we cannot find ourselves and offer our gifts, it affects us all. What I share in this workbook are the directions to follow and create your own individual foundation. Tools to reframe the inner obstacles in the mind. In the following pages, are the simple structures to establish a connection to access your intuitive self. Everyone has a back story, for many the challenges and mistakes in our lives have opened us up to the possibility of a spiritual life and our own value. If you are here, consider that you're ready to open these doors.

2-CREATING YOUR SPACE

Photo by Kir Noel /Maine coast

Your first step is creating a private

sacred space, that you will be using for five

minutes twice a day. It needs to be a place where you can leave a few items undisturbed. It can be in any area, no matter how small. One of my students used a nightstand drawer as she had young children. This is a space to bring you a feeling of safety and self-care. Select and place objects in your space that help you to connect to these feelings. In addition, place a small clear bowl of water that you can refill each morning. Put images and items in your sacred space that connect you to the elements in your life that ground you.

Here are some examples of what people have used. Feathers, photos, crystals, writing, poems, a scarf, a piece of jewelry from a loved one, a piece of wood, flowers, a mala, stones sand.

Once you have created the space, you are ready to write an intention.

3-INTENTION SETTING

My Alter

Our intuitive mind is the receptive part of us. In many ways it is limitless and porous. Because of this, creating a boundary and stability are a basic requirement. What does that mean? Basically, it follows the principal- *be careful of what you wish for you, you might get it.* Words are the keys to unlocking the access to your truth. When I teach this at a retreat, I instruct students to take their time. It's always important to ask, what do you want this work to create in your life and how do you wish it to impact those around you? Often, we'll take a session to discuss our intentions in pairs. I see it as the structure to build our growth on, a cornerstone of our foundation.

Here are some examples-

I wish to be open to my true self, beyond my ego mind.

I am willing to let go of any attitude, belief or behavior that blocks me.

I am open to all; I am and ready to release my delusions.

I seek to live in the light of my path.

Once you have your intention, write it down and place it on the space you'll practice in. The next focus will be on establishing a space to find your clarity that is grounded and safe. We are mostly water, and we have energy which all our cells hold. The concept is illustrated by how a wire maintains electrical integrity. It must have a coating on it, or it would encounter interference and dissipate. Your ability to have a clear consistent connection, is related to you being grounded. For this purpose, I recommend you have some items near you that offer a feeling of spiritual grounding.

Examples of this are -

a picture of a friend or family member that you feel is a guide to you.

an image from your spiritual tradition

a historical figure you admire.

a saint

an animal

Once you have these items, place them in your sacred space.

4–OPENING THE DOOR

Every morning for five minutes, sit in front of the alter you created. Read your intention so you can put this into your mind for the day. I offer you a simple meditation below to bring you to an interconnected space. This will allow you to be more receptive to your daily insights. You can say this meditation out loud or record it and listen to it each morning. This is one way to bring the connected self into focus. Feel free to use any meditation you find for yourself. It is important you have a method to get grounded and connected to start your day.

A meditation -
You are seated on a warm sandy beach as the sun is rising. You close your eyes, look inside yourself and enter your

heart center. There you see a warm glowing light, as you see this light it begins to expand outwardly to fill your head, chest, legs, and arms until you are filled. Then this light begins to radiate outwardly. Like a million-year-old oak tree, your body upwardly reaches out into the space around you and into the earth. Your roots expand. Branches and roots that are connected to every living being on earth. You can see light in every living being on earth. This connection is limitless. Sit in the unlimited connected self you are.

5-LOOKING

With these elements you can begin the first day's process. Sit in the space you created and read your intention. Try to mentally carry this awareness throughout the day. At the end of each day write down what you've observed. Look at the moments of strong emotions, note key observations of what you experienced throughout the day, so that you can recall it later. Once you have completed this for a week, go into the notes and write in each category what repeats for you.

Next begin to write questions you have that are based on your patterns. There may be only one or perhaps none. If there are no questions continue and do the next week of observation. Write down questions as they arise, and each morning ask for the teaching in these to be presented to you.

As you continue to receive information include these in your daily writing. This may expand beyond the space in this notebook. These are the jewels that will light your way to yourself. There will be a new level of awareness doing this practice daily and a subsequent change in attitude.[1]

1.Note: As you complete this practice you may wish to contact me to further your studies. Go to my website healingabody.com to write me and in notes reference The Workbook as the reason you are contacting me.

Following are the pages for the next twelve weeks. I recommend you take a weekly rest from doing these.

Wednesday.

04/17/24

Date:

WEEKLY

MINDFULNESS

JOURNAL

....

....

....

....

....

....

....

....

....

....

....

....

....

....

Date:

WEEKLY MINDFULNESS JOURNAL

....

....

....

....

....

....

....

....

....

....

....

....

Notes–

My fears

Self-criticism

Date:

WEEKLY MINDFULNESS JOURNAL

....

....

....

....

....

....

....

....

....

....

....

....

Notes–

My fears

Self-criticism

Date:

WEEKLY

MINDFULNESS

JOURNAL

....

....

....

....

....

....

....

....

....

....

....

....

Notes-

My fears

Self-criticism

Date:

WEEKLY MINDFULNESS JOURNAL

....

....

....

....

....

....

....

....

....

....

....

....

Notes–

My fears

Self-criticism

Date:

WEEKLY

MINDFULNESS

JOURNAL

Notes–

My fears

Self-criticism

Date:

WEEKLY
MINDFULNESS
JOURNAL

....

....

....

....

....

....

....

....

....

....

....

....

Notes–

My fears

Self-criticism

Date:

WEEKLY
MINDFULNESS
JOURNAL

....

....

....

....

....

....

....

....

....

....

....

....

Notes–

My fears

Self-criticism

Date:

WEEKLY MINDFULNESS JOURNAL

....

....

....

....

....

....

....

....

....

....

....

....

Notes–

My fears

Self-criticism

Date:

WEEKLY
MINDFULNESS
JOURNAL

....
....
....
....
....
....
....
....
....
....
....
....

Notes–

My fears

Self-criticism

Date:

WEEKLY MINDFULNESS JOURNAL

....

....

....

....

....

....

....

....

....

....

....

....

....

....

Notes–

My fears

Self-criticism

After completing these practices, if you decide you want to further your studies, please contact me.

Go to my website **healingabody.com** and use the question form. Indicate that you have been using the workbook. I look forward to hearing from you.

Kir Noel is a practicing Medical Intuitive. She has worked alongside physicians in all fields of medicine for over 25 years. She is a member of KTD a Tibetan Buddhist monastery in Woodstock, N.Y. Her passion is to help others find their path.

This is her first workbook.

Kir Noel

Printed in the USA
CPSIA information can be obtained
at www.ICGtesting.com
JSHW042033120124
55336JS00001B/1